Food and
Cooking

Ready, Steady, Play!

Series Editor: Sandy Green

Guaranteed fun for children and practitioners alike, the Ready, Steady, Play! series provides lively and stimulating activities for children.

Each book focuses on one specific aspect of play offering clear and detailed guidance on how to plan and enjoy wonderful play experiences with minimum fuss and maximum success.

Each book in the Ready, Steady, Play! series includes advice on:

- How to prepare the children and the play space
- What equipment and materials are needed
- How much time is needed to prepare and carry out the activity
- How many staff are required
- How to communicate with parents and colleagues

Ready, Steady, Play! helps you to:

- Develop activities easily, using suggested guidelines
- Ensure that health and safety issues are taken into account
- Plan play that links to the early years curriculum
- Broaden your understanding of early years issues

Early years practitioners and students on early years courses and parents looking for simple, excellent ideas for creative play will love these books!

Other titles in the series

Books, Stories and Puppets 1-84312-148-4 Green
Construction 1-84312-098-4 Boyd
Creativity 1-84312-076-3 Green
Displays and Interest Tables 1-84312-267-7 Olpin
Festivals 1-84312-101-8 Hewitson
Music and Singing 1-84312-276-6 Green
Nature, Living and Growing 1-84312-114-X Harper
Play Using Natural Materials 1-84312-099-2 Howe
Role Play 1-84312-147-6 Green

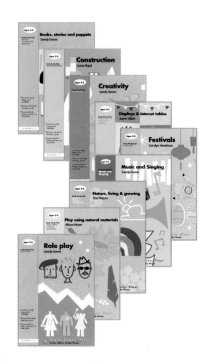

Contents

Food and Cooking

Welcome to *Food and Cooking*, an exciting new publication which is part of the Ready, Steady, Play! series.

Get ready to enjoy a range of activities with your children, which will stimulate their all-round development.

The Ready, Steady, Play! books will help boost the confidence of new practitioners by providing informative and fun ideas to support planning and preparation. The series will also consolidate and extend learning for the more experienced practitioner. Attention is drawn to health and safety, and the role of the adult is addressed.

How to use this book

Food and Cooking is divided into five main sections.

Section 1 provides a range of background information on using food as a focus of learning. It also provides a brief outline of nutrition, together with information on a variety of special dietary requirements.

Section 2 presents visual material to stimulate discussion with children in a group setting or one to one. Here you will find photographs of fruits, vegetables and breads from around the world, together with pages of ingredients to discuss with the children, encouraging them to think what they could make with them.

The activity section encourages practitioners to help children explore food through a range of different approaches, and using all of their senses, for example, cooking, handling, smelling, replicating and exploring the similarities and differences between foods. These activities primarily use foods that are readily available and all activities have easy-to-follow guidelines.

Section 4 provides ideas for attractive snacks and meals to stimulate interest in food if you are working with a child who is a reluctant eater. There are also ideas suitable for picnics and parties.

The photocopiable pages at the end of the book provide relevant activities for children to enjoy and complete, all based on foods familiar to most families. These pages build on the learning aims of the set activities, or follow on from the discussion pages in Section 1, and may be used as evidence of developing skills and understanding, or to involve parents in what their child has been learning.

So read on, and enjoy ... Ready, Steady, Play!

Sandy Green
Series editor

Acknowledgements

Thanks are due to Sainsbury's supermarket, Bath, for donating a range of foods for the photographs in this book. Also to John for his ongoing support, and to Nina Stibbe of David Fulton Publishers for her enthusiasm as a photographer. Also to GALT for the use of pictures from their catalogue.

To my granddaughter Jasmine: thank you for always being willing to play – making items for and with Granny.

Series acknowledgement

The series editor would like to thank the children, parents and staff at:

- The Nursery, Wadebridge Community Primary School, Wadebridge, Cornwall
- Happy Days Day Nursery, Wadebridge, Cornwall
- Snapdragons Nursery, Weston, Bath, Somerset
- Snapdragons Nursery, Grosvenor, Bath, Somerset
- Tadpoles Nursery, Combe Down, Bath, Somerset

for allowing us to take photographs of their excellent provision, resources and displays.

Also to John and Jake Green, Jasmine and Eva for their help throughout the series, and to Paul Isbell at David Fulton Publishers for his patience, enthusiasm and support.

Introduction

Using food as a focus of learning

When presenting activities involving food within early years settings, there will be opportunities to help influence children's attitudes to food and to eating, and to build on their understanding of the importance of eating healthily. The social side of sharing a meal or snack time is not something experienced by all children, as many families today eat in shifts or in front of the television. Enjoying food together offers a chance for discussion of likes and dislikes and conversation in general.

It is important that children are allowed to explore food with each of their senses, to handle, smell and taste a variety of foods, many of which they may not see at home, always being aware of the need to check for food allergies and intolerances in advance. Food is a vital part of daily living, and encouraging children to explore and experiment with food can help set good eating habits for the future.

Introducing food in both its raw and cooked state can help children begin to understand the science of cooking, as they observe the changes that occur during the cooking process. Whenever practical, let them observe food at each stage.

Encouragement to try new foods is important, but practitioners need to accept that some children will only wish to observe, and that some children have restrictions due to medical or cultural necessity (see pages 6–10). Alternative activities or foods should be provided for these children.

Within each activity in this book there is a list of suggested vocabulary and discussion ideas, and they are exactly that – suggestions. They should not be seen as prescriptive or comprehensive. They are provided to help guide new and less experienced practitioners in how to introduce and enhance language use through practical situations, and to prompt and consolidate language use for more experienced practitioners.

The snack and meal ideas set out in Section 4 are quick and easy to present, particularly if catering for small numbers. They provide interest for children who are not keen on eating, taking some of the attention away from the food itself.

In summary we can say that including food-related activities as part of the early years curriculum provides children with the following key learning opportunities:

■ the opportunity to try new tastes and textures;
■ the opportunity for a shared social experience;
■ enhanced understanding of where food comes from and how it is prepared;

- exploration and investigation opportunities;
- further development of fine motor skills;
- language development through discussion and questioning as an individual, either one to one with an adult or within a group situation;
- concentration skills as they focus on the task they are completing;
- emotional satisfaction regarding effort and achievement.

Health and safety

Attention to health and safety is vital when working with food. Relevant points to be considered have been indicated for each of the activities in this book. A summary of these is as follows:

- Ensure that surfaces are always clean when preparing food.
- Ensure that children wash their hands thoroughly before all food activities.
- Be seen to wash your hands well too, even if you have already done so.
- Always maintain appropriate adult–child ratios.
- Limit numbers, particularly when closer supervision is needed (e.g. when using knives).
- Be aware of food allergies and intolerances, and plan in advance to provide alternatives for any affected children.
- Carefully supervise use of all sharp implements (e.g. knives, peelers, graters).
- Remember that the cooker should be used only by the adults.
- Cooking ingredients should be packed away carefully to avoid contamination.

The adult role

As well as ensuring a healthy and safe environment during food activities and cooking, the adult has other important roles too. These include:

- Planning activities carefully, ensuring an anti-discriminatory approach is taken at all times.
- Providing appropriate utensils for each activity.
- Providing sufficient utensils and resources to achieve a satisfying activity.

- Giving praise and encouragement.
- Supporting learning through challenge and stimulation.
- Encouraging language use and vocabulary extension through discussion and open questioning.
- Observing children and assessing their progress.
- Providing extension activities where appropriate, and as time allows.

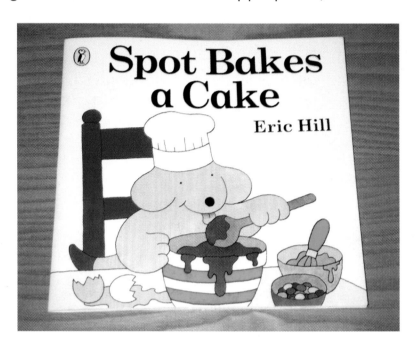

Nutrition

Most health and nutrition professionals agree that what young children eat will not only affect their growth and development but will also impact on their lives as adults. Encouraging children to eat well and to have a healthy attitude to food will help them make sensible choices for themselves.

Use the photographs on pages 16–29 to discuss with children what foods they eat, and how these foods help them in their growth and bodily health. Ask which foods they would choose and why.

There are four main food groups, plus fats. It is important that children receive a balanced amount from these groups.

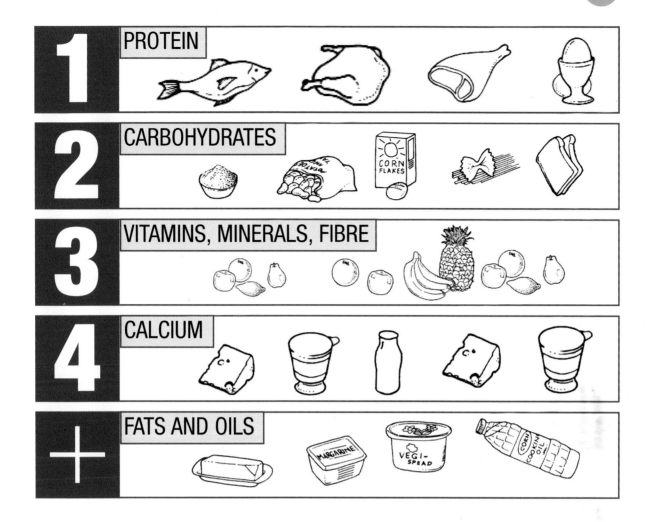

Nutritionists suggest the following guidelines for children each day:

- Proteins   Two portions
- Carbohydrates   Five portions
- Vitamins, minerals and fibre   Five portions
- Calcium   Four portions
- Fats and oils   To be offered from time to time.

Young children should be drinking one pint of milk each day, plus other fluids.

Eating five portions of fruit and vegetables each day is fine in theory, but not always so easy in practice. If you are providing for a child who is not so keen on fruit and vegetables, try to make them more attractive.

Try:

- Giving them a bowl of bite-size pieces of fruits and crunchy vegetables.
- Focusing on providing the most brightly coloured fresh foods.
- Adding fresh fruit to jelly.
- Blending vegetables into casseroles, so they are 'hidden' in the gravy.
- Providing dried fruit such as whole apricots for snack time.
- Keeping an interesting fruit bowl whenever possible.
- To be seen to enjoy fruit and vegetables yourself.

Use the activity on page 52 to help children make food choices for each food group.

Special diets

When providing meals for children, and when planning cooking or food-based activities, parties and picnics, cultural rules regarding diet must be taken into consideration. The following chart shows some of the commonly followed choices made by a range of cultures. It is always important that practitioners check details with each child's parent or carer.

'Some' means that some people within a religious group would find these foods acceptable.

	Jewish	Hindu[1]	Sikh[1]	Muslim	Buddhist	Rastafarian[2]
Eggs	No blood spots	Some	Yes	Yes	Some	Some
Milk/yoghurt	Not with meat	Yes	Yes	Yes	Yes	Some
Cheese	Not with meat	Some	Some	Possibly	Yes	Some
Chicken	Kosher	Some	Some	Halal	No	Some
Mutton/lamb	Kosher	Some	Yes	Halal	No	Some
Beef and beef products	Kosher	No	No	Halal	No	Some
Pork and pork products	No	No	Rarely	No	No	No

	Jewish	Hindu[1]	Sikh[1]	Muslim	Buddhist	Rastafarian[2]
Fish	With fins and scales	With fins and scales	Some	Some	Some	Yes
Shellfish	No	Some	Some	Some	No	No
Butter/ghee	Kosher	Some	Some	Some	No	Some
Lard	No	No	No	No	No	No
Cereal foods	Yes	Yes	Yes	Yes	Yes	Yes
Nuts/pulses	Yes	Yes	Yes	Yes	Yes	Yes
Fruits/vegetables	Yes	Yes[3]	Yes	Yes	Yes	Yes
Fasting[4]	Yes	Yes	Yes	Yes	Yes	Yes

Source: Caroline Walker Trust

1 Strict Hindus and Sikhs will not eat eggs, meat, fish and some fats
2 Some Rastafarians are vegan.
3 Jains have restrictions on some vegetable foods. Check with the individuals.
4 Fasting is unlikely to apply to young children.

Children need to be helped to explore and enjoy new tastes and textures with confidence. It is important that records of food allergies and intolerance are kept updated and that all staff can access the information as necessary.

Vegetarian diets

Vegetarian diets do not include meat or (usually) fish. Since meat and fish are a high source of protein in non-vegetarian diets, it is important that children following a vegetarian diet receive sufficient protein through other sources (milk, cheese, eggs, beans, legumes, cereal products). If working with vegetarian children it is important that you are aware of 'hidden' animal products within many cooking fats and gelatine.

Vegan diets

People following a vegan diet accept no produce of animals whatsoever. Naturally this not only rules out meat and fish, but also excludes foods such as milk, cheese, honey and eggs. Achieving the appropriate balance of proteins in a child's diet needs to be managed carefully, with an emphasis often placed on the inclusion of whole grains (e.g. brown rice, barley, millet, couscous), legumes (e.g. beans, chickpeas, tofu, mungs, alfalfa sprouts, lentils), and nuts and seeds (e.g. sunflower, tahini, nut butters).

It should be remembered that the inclusion of nuts in a young child's diet is not recommended by many health professionals due to the increased potential for developing nut allergy. In addition, most early years settings do not allow any nut-based products to be brought into the setting by children or included in cooking activities and meals. This helps to avoid the risk of any child already having an identified nut allergy coming into accidental contact with a sensitive food source. Advice from a vegan child's parents will need to be taken.

Remember:

Cooking activities do not always have to be of the cake and biscuit variety. Refer to pages 38 and 62 as examples of suitable activities found in this book.

Gluten intolerance – Coeliac disease

Coeliac disease is a condition in which the individual is unable to tolerate the protein gluten, which is found in wheat, barley, rye and oats. It affects the lining of the small intestine, flattening the 'finger-like' villi of the intestine's absorbency surface and therefore lessening the ability to absorb goodness from food. A distended stomach, diarrhoea and failure to thrive are often the earliest signs. There is a growing awareness of this condition, with more and more people being diagnosed as gluten intolerant each year.

Gluten is often a hidden ingredient, and many processed foods contain it as it is a binding agent. Other foods come into contact with gluten during the manufacturing process, through flour on conveyer belts. It is important that guidance is taken from parents and carers regarding what a child with the condition can and cannot eat.

Most parents will be accustomed to providing alternatives for their child, but you should try to accommodate their needs whenever possible. Often cooking activities can be carried out just as easily using chickpea flour, rice flour or a ready prepared gluten-free flour mix (most main supermarkets stock a brand) without losing any of the flavour, texture and appearance of the 'normal' item.

Playdough can easily be made from gluten-free flour (see page 13 for a special recipe). This is important when working with very young children who may put doughy hands into their mouths. In children with an extreme sensitivity, handling foods containing gluten is also a problem, and therefore gluten-free playdough becomes vital.

Snack time, parties and picnics can often be the most difficult to cater for. Including plenty of fresh foods such as fruit, crunchy vegetables and salad items can help. Try including ideas such as the fruit kebabs on page 48.

Lactose intolerance

This is a condition in which the child is unable to tolerate a sugar found in milk. It causes severe diarrhoea and abdominal pain, and children fail to thrive properly. It often means the child will need to drink soya milk, and to eat foods made with soya-based products. Advice from parents regarding what a child can and cannot eat should be sought. Soya milk may be used successfully to make the fruit smoothies on page 62.

Diabetes in children

Children with type 1 diabetes (diabetes mellitus) need to maintain a careful balance of their blood glucose levels. This is achieved by both diet and insulin, which are determined by levels of planned and unexpected exercise. Each child has a carefully planned diet and insulin routine, and their care is overseen by a specialist diabetic health professional.

Too much exercise or insulin, or a missed meal or snack, can result in **hypoglycaemia** (low levels of glucose in the blood), causing dizziness, pallor, sweating and confusion. Without treatment the child can become unconscious, needing urgent medical help. The symptoms can develop quickly.

Practitioners should always have immediate access to easily absorbed sugary foods (glucose tablets, biscuits, sugar cubes or a carton of juice) for such emergencies. These should also be taken out on any trips away from the setting.

Less exercise than usual, a lack of insulin, too much carbohydrate food, sudden excitement or anxiety, or an infection, can result in **hyperglycaemia** (higher than usual levels of glucose in the blood). This occurs more slowly, with the child becoming sleepy, thirsty and passing a large volume of urine. Again, intervention is needed, usually an insulin injection, to avoid loss of consciousness.

Children with diabetes should never be kept waiting for their meals and snacks. Advice should be sought from their parents, and any concerns reported to them.

Playdough

Playing with playdough is an activity enjoyed by most young children. It should ideally be offered as an unstructured, freeplay activity without adult direction.

It also makes a wonderful cooking activity, and may be adjusted to include a variety of smells and textures.

It is important that practitioners encourage children to handle the dough directly, without always using cutters and rolling-pins. This helps them to engage directly with it.

The role of the adult at the dough table is to discuss with the children what they are doing, encouraging vocabulary which describes their experience (e.g. mould, shape, squeeze, roll).

Changing the children's experience by mixing items such as jumbo oats into the dough gives an alternative visual and tactile stimulus. Adding a food essence such as lemon can stimulate their olfactory senses too (see scented dough activity on page 58).

It should be remembered that the inclusion of oats is not appropriate in gluten-free playdough (see special recipe on page 13), as many children with the gluten intolerance condition coeliac also have an intolerance to oats.

Making playdough – cooked recipe

Cooked playdough probably lasts longer than any other type of dough. However, it should be replaced regularly, particularly if a viral infection has entered the setting.

Ingredients

2 cups flour
1 cup salt
2 cups water
2 tablespoons cooking oil (sunflower or vegetable)
2 teaspoons cream of tartar
1 teaspoon food colouring (optional)

Method

1. Place all the ingredients in a pan.
2. Cook over a gentle heat, stirring continuously.
3. When the dough mixture 'comes away' from the sides of the pan, it is ready.
4. Turn the dough on to a board.
5. Knead well to remove any lumps.
6. When cool, store in an airtight container in the refrigerator.

Making playdough – uncooked recipes

Each of the following recipes is ideal for making with children.

Recipe 1 – Non-stretchy dough

Ingredients

1.5 kg plain flour
750 g cooking salt
Approximately 750 ml water

Method

1. Combine the flour and salt in a large bowl.
2. Gradually add the water.
3. Knead well to ensure a smooth texture.

This dough will break cleanly. It holds its shape well, and can be pulled apart in small pieces and squashed back together again. It does not stretch.

Recipe 2 – stretchy dough

Ingredients

1.5 kg self-raising flour
Approximately 750 ml water
No salt

Method

1. Gradually add the water to the flour.
2. Knead the dough well to obtain a very smooth consistency.

This dough is stretchy and does not break into clean 'chunks'. It can be stretched into a 'dough rope' and swung gently. If holes are poked into this type of dough, they will gradually fill up again.

Recipe 3 – super stretchy dough

Ingredients

1.5 kg strong bread flour
Water
No salt

Method

1. Gradually add the water to the flour.
2. Knead well to obtain a very smooth consistency.

This dough feels like strong elastic. It can be stretched into long lengths and swung like a lasso!

Making playdough – A gluten-free recipe

Children who have the condition coeliac have an intolerance to the substance gluten which is found in wheat, barley, rye and oats. For some, the effects are seen only when they have eaten something containing these foods, but for others, simply handling the ingredients can cause them problems.

It is important to remember that playdough is usually made with wheat-based flour and is therefore not suitable for a child with coeliac. The following recipe offers a useful alternative that can be safely used by coeliac and non-coeliac children.

Remember:

Although adding textures to playdough can enhance the experience for the children, textures such as oats should not be included in this recipe.

Ingredients

1 cup riceflour
1 cup cornflour
1 cup salt
4 teaspoons cream of tartar
2 cups water
2 tablespoons vegetable oil
Food colouring (optional)

Method

1. Place all the ingredients together in a saucepan.
2. Stir well while cooking over a gentle heat.
3. Continue to stir. The mixture will change from a runny consistency to a firmer consistency.
4. Remove pan from the heat and turn the dough on to a board.
5. Knead the dough well to get a smooth texture throughout.
6. When cool, place dough in a plastic container and store in the refrigerator until required.

Playdough keeps well if refrigerated between uses, but should be regularly replaced for hygiene reasons, particularly if an infectious illness has entered the setting.

Discussion resources

The following section provides a range of photographs of different foods to stimulate discussion with children, broadening their knowledge of fruits, vegetables and other foods, and offering ideal opportunities to emphasise the importance of a healthy diet.

- fruit
- vegetables
- breads
- cooking ingredients

Fruit

Apple

Orange

Pear

Banana

Plum

Grape

Peach

Strawberry

Kiwi

Mango and pawpaw

Fig

Avocado

Lime

Grapefruit

Lemon

Coconut

Melon

Pineapple

Vegetables

Tomato

Lettuce

Radish

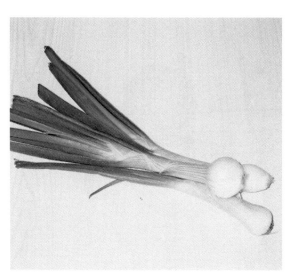

Spring onion

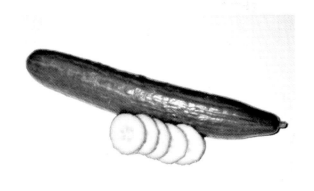

Cucumber

Celery

Chinese leaf

Cress

Potato

Carrot

Swede

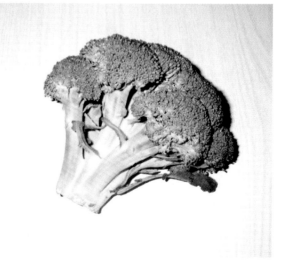

Broccoli

Spinach

Onion

Cabbage

Cauliflower

Aubergine

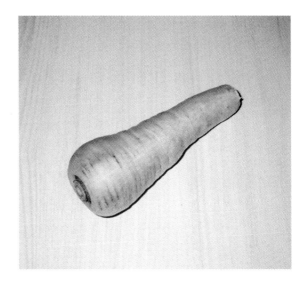

Parsnip

Sprout

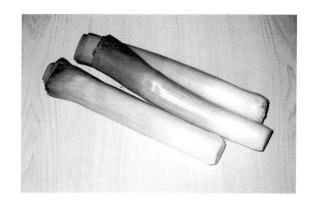

Leek

Squash

Mushroom

Chilli

Fennel

Garlic

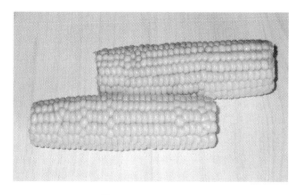

Sweetcorn

Pea

Pepper

Courgette

Asparagus

Sweet potato

Runner bean

Green bean

Herbs

Sweet basil

Sage

Parsley

Rosemary

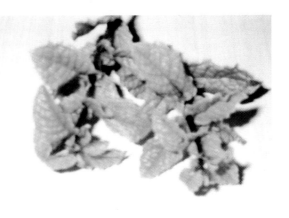

Mint

Breads

White loaf

Sliced loaf

Baguette

Wholemeal roll

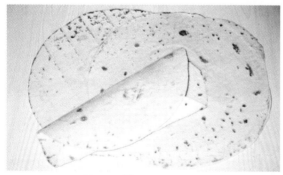

Tortilla wrap

Pitta bread

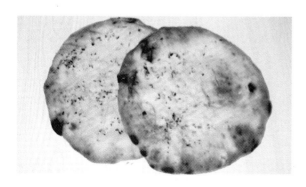

Naan bread

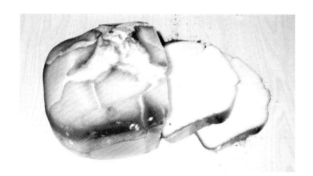

Focaccia

What could we make with these ingredients?

Margarine

Sugar

Egg

Flour

Dried fruit

Glacé cherry

What could we make here?

Slices of bread

Margarine

Cheese

Cucumber

Lettuce

Sliced tomato

Activities

The following pages contain twenty different activities either cooking with or involving food. Each activity follows a standard format to ensure ease of planning and implementation:

- the resources needed
- the aim(s)/concept(s)
- the process
- group size
- health and safety
- discussion ideas/language
- extension ideas
- links to the Foundation Stage Curriculum.

Key to Foundation Stage Curriculum abbreviations:

SS   Stepping stones

ELG   Early Learning goals

PSE   Personal, social and emotional development

CLL   Communication, language and literacy

MD   Mathematical development

KUW   Knowledge and understanding of the world

PD   Physical development

CD   Creative development

ACTIVITY

1 Special eggs

Resources you will need:

- An already hard-boiled egg
- A saucepan of water
- Access to a cooker (adults only)
- An egg for each child (the eggs may be cooked in advance)
- Containers of cold water
- Food dyes (or natural dyes such as tea)
- Metal spoons
- Access to a refrigerator
- Handwashing facilities nearby

Aim/concept

- For children to enjoy a 'magical' change, learning about cause and effect

Process

Part 1

- Show the children the prepared egg, and encourage them to explain how it became hard boiled.
- Let each child carefully put an egg into the pan of cold water and then explain that you will take the eggs to be boiled for about twenty minutes to achieve a 'hard-boiled' state (in a cooking area away from the children).
- Allow eggs to cool so they can be handled.

Part 2

- Give each child a hard-boiled egg and a spoon, and let them tap gently around the egg to make it crack.
- Let the children add food colouring to a range of containers of water.
- Each child chooses which colour container they wish to add their egg to.
- Place containers in a refrigerator overnight.

Next day

- Let the children peel the shells off their eggs to find the marbled effect, and enjoy them at snack or lunch time.

Vocabulary/discussion

- Discuss what happened, how, and why
- Encourage vocabulary linked to change: hardened, solidified, altered, different, boiled, cooked
- Talk about the patterns and how they were made: tapped, bashed, cracked, marbled, veined
- Talk about colour names and any difference in the colours between dye and egg colours (e.g. black dye produces purplish eggs)

Group size

6–8

Extension ideas

1. Make natural dyes using tea, beetroot and so on.
2. Do 'marbling' painting.
3. Use the eggs to make 'exciting' sandwiches (see page 74 for more ideas).

Links to Foundation Stage Curriculum

CLL	Use talk to connect ideas, explain what is happening and anticipate what might happen next (SS)
ELG	Use talk to organise, sequence and clarify thinking, ideas, feelings and events
KUW	Talk about what is seen and what is happening (SS)
ELG	Ask questions about why things happen and how things work
CD	Show an interest in what they see, hear, smell, touch and feel (SS)
	Use body language, gestures, facial expressions or words to indicate (SS) personal satisfaction or frustration.
ELG	Respond in a variety of ways to what they see, hear, smell, touch and feel

Health and safety

⚠ Only adults to have access to kitchen and pans of hot water
⚠ Be aware of allergies to eggs
⚠ Children with skin complaints such as eczema may need to wear disposable gloves because of the dyes

ACTIVITY 2 What can you smell?

Resources you will need

- A range of small pots (preferably) with lids (film canisters are ideal)
- A variety of strong-smelling food items to hide in the pots
- Pictures of each item

Aim/concept

- To help children identify foods using their sense of smell

Process

- Prepare the 'scented' pots in advance, making a few holes in the lid and giving each pot a number.
- Make sure you know which food item is in each number pot.
- Talk to the children about their sense of smell, asking them what sort of smells they like and dislike. Keep them focused on food items.
- Talk about the strength of smells – subtle, strong, fragrant, spicy.
- Show the children your range of pots.
- Let the children explore the pots, smelling them each in turn, encouraging discussion, comparison and questions.
- Can the children guess what is making each smell?

Either:
- Give the children the picture to hold of all the smells they get right – who gets the most? – or:
- Lay out the pictures where all the children can see them. Which pots can they match correctly to each picture?

Vocabulary/discussion

- Talk about the strength of smells, using vocabulary such as mild, subtle, strong, fragrant, spicy, pungent
- Talk about likes and dislikes, which smells/foods the children have tasted. Can they describe tastes linked to smells (e.g. citrus fruits are tangy (taste) and pungent (smell)?

Group size

6–8

Extension ideas

1. Link to a topic on the senses.
2. Make a display of likes and dislikes, using pictures or examples (sprigs of plants, herbs).
3. Make scented playdough (see page 58)
4. Talk about the sense of smell in animals and its importance to them.

Links to Foundation Stage Curriculum

CLL Extend vocabulary, especially by grouping and naming (SS)

ELG Extend their vocabulary, exploring the meanings and sounds of new words

KUW Examine objects and living things to find out more about them (SS)

ELG Investigate objects and materials by using all of their senses as appropriate

CD Show an interest in what they see, hear, smell, touch and feel (SS)

ELG Respond in a variety of ways to what they see, hear, smell, touch and feel

Health and safety

⚠ Ensure all items used are safe
⚠ Be aware of any allergies

ACTIVITY

3 # Making sandwiches

Resources you will need

- Slices of bread
- Margarine
- Round-ended knives
- Plates
- A variety of food choices for the sandwich fillings (e.g. marmite, paste, cream cheese, slices of cheese, slices of cucumber and tomato, jam)
- Pastry cutters (optional)

Aim/concept

- For children to make choices and develop manipulative skills while preparing their own snacks

Process

- Take the children to wash their hands. Let them see you wash yours too.
- Talk to the children about sandwiches, asking them about their likes and dislikes, and when they usually eat sandwiches.
- Talk about hygiene when handling food.
- Show the children how you clean the table with an anti-bacterial product.
- Show the children how to spread the margarine, holding the knife at a flattened angle.
- Help the children to cut their slice of bread in half, so they can make two different choices.
- Encourage the children to choose both a filling that they know they like, and one so that they can try a new taste.
- Encourage sharing and passing of items around the table.
- When the sandwich fillings have been added, help the children to match up the top slices, again having cut a slice of bread in half.
- Help the children to either cut their sandwiches into rectangles, squares or triangles, or let them use the pastry cutters.
- Encourage the children to talk about their sandwiches during snack time, what did they taste like: which did they like best and why?

Vocabulary/discussion

- Encourage words to describe the sandwich fillings – sweet, savoury, salty, creamy, crunchy, cold, yummy
- Talk about the skills involved in sandwich making – spreading, cutting
- Refer to food names, colours, shape names
- Talk about when we eat sandwiches – lunch, snack time, parties, picnics

Group size

4

Extension ideas

1. Prepare sandwiches for a picnic and take them outside to eat on a nice day.
2. Make marmalade sandwiches and link them to the Paddington Bear stories by Michael Bond, or read *The Giant Jam Sandwich* by John Vernon Lord and Janet Burroway.
3. Make paper sandwiches for a display on picnics, using pictures of food from magazines as the fillings.

Links to Foundation Stage Curriculum

CLL Use simple statements and questions, often linked to gesture (SS)

ELG Interact with others, negotiating plans and activities and taking turns in conversation

KUW Describe simple features of objects and events (SS)

ELG Investigate objects and materials by using all their senses as appropriate

PD Engage in activities requiring hand–eye coordination (SS)

ELG Handle tools, objects, construction and malleable materials safely and with increasing control

Health and safety

⚠ Hygiene issues regarding handwashing and not touching mouths and faces when handling food

⚠ Be aware of any food allergies (e.g. to fish (pastes), eggs)

⚠ Ensure that no child eats any food that is not allowed to them due to cultural restrictions

⚠ Use only round-ended knives for spreading

⚠ Each child to have their own utensils

ACTIVITY 4 Preparing a fruit salad

Resources you will need

- A chopping board for each child
- A round-ended knife for each child
- Spoons
- A large plastic bowl
- A small bowl for each child
- A jug, or jugs of juice
- A selection of fruits (it is cheaper if you select seasonal fruits); try using apples, grapes, satsumas, raspberries, melon, pineapple, mango, banana. Star fruit also look super. Kiwi fruit are best avoided due to allergic reactions in some children

Aim/concept

- To explore various features of a range of fruits, observing, tasting and combining them within a fruit salad

Process

- Take the children to wash their hands, and be seen to wash yours too.
- Explore the fruits with the children, looking at their colour and shape, and feeling the different textures of their skins.
- Discuss with the children the seeds, stones and so on, explaining how these can help to produce the next crop of fruit.
- Give the children pieces of each fruit to smell and taste.
- Encourage the children to describe the features of each fruit, and say which they like and dislike.

Either:
- Let the children choose fruit to cut up for a communal fruit salad, and then serve it out into individual bowls, *or:*
- Ask them to choose four fruits for their own personal salad.
- Carefully supervise the use of knives.
- Let each child add a little juice to their bowl.
- Enjoy eating the salad together, discussing and describing taste and texture to each other.

Vocabulary/ discussion

- Discuss the fruit, drawing the children's attention to each of the senses; what do the fruits look like? How do they feel? What do they smell like? What do they taste like?
- Ask the children to identify colours, shades and depth of colour, and introduce relevant terms to describe the skin of the fruit, such as pitted (orange), spiky (pineapple), velvety (peach), rubbery (banana).
- Talk about the seeds of each fruit, their shape, texture and size.
- Use terms such as peeling, cutting, slicing, sweet, sour, juicy, crunchy.

Group size

6

Extension ideas

1. Make fruit drinks instead, choosing fruits and using a blender (adult use only), or try the fruit smoothies on page 62.
2. Wash the seeds, pips and stones and sort by elected features.
3. Print using fruits (see page 60).
4. Read the story *Oliver's Fruit Salad* by Vivian French.
5. Read the story *Mr Rabbit and the Lovely Present* by Charlotte Zolotow, illustrated by Maurice Sendak.
6. Plant seeds and pips and see if they grow.

Links to Foundation Stage Curriculum

KUW Examine objects and living things to find out more about them (SS)

ELG Find out about, and identify, some features of living things, objects and events they observe

PD Use one-handed tools and equipment (SS)

SS Understand that tools and equipment have to be used safely (SS)

ELG Handle tools, objects, construction and malleable materials safely and with increasing control

CD Show an interest in what they see, hear, smell, touch and feel (SS)

SS Further explore an experience, using a range of senses (SS)

ELG Respond in a variety of ways to what they see, hear, smell, touch and feel

Health and safety

⚠ Handwashing
⚠ Careful supervision of knife use
⚠ Be aware of food allergies
⚠ Ensure seeds, pips and stones are not eaten

ACTIVITY 5 Making cakes

Resources you will need

- Mixing bowl
- Wooden spoons
- Scales
- Copies of photocopiable recipe (see page 93 (optional))
- Ingredients for making cakes, as set out in recipe
- Timer (if available)

Aim/concept

- To explore the science of combining ingredients, noting any changes

Process

- Take the children to wash their hands. Be seen to wash yours too.
- Talk to the children about the ingredients, each in turn – where they come from, how they may be used, if/how/when they usually eat them.
- According to what you have chosen, explain to the children the sorts of cakes they will be making (see page 94 for ideas).
- If using the recipe card, talk it through with the children.
- Help them follow the guidance on the recipe card, letting them take the lead as much as possible.

Alternatively...
- Guide the children through the cake-making process, encouraging them to take turns and share the adding, mixing and so on.
- Talk about measurements, amounts and so on.
- Talk to the children about the ingredients and how they are changing during the cake-making process.
- When mixed, take the cakes to the kitchen, explaining to the children how long the cakes will take to cook. Set a timer if possible.
- While the cakes are cooking (adults only near cookers) and cooling, talk to the children about how they will decorate their cakes.
- They could draw their ideas on circles of paper, or use the photocopiable cake template on page 91 to get ideas.

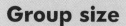

Vocabulary/ discussion

- Use vocabulary to name the ingredients, and discuss their origins and uses
- Talk about the changes seen during the cooking process, referring to words such as dry, liquid, runny, creamy, thickened, mixed, combined, cook, bake, change, altered and so on
- Compare weights and amounts, and talk about measurements, numbers of eggs, spoonfuls and so on

Group size

4–6

Extension ideas

1. Have an impromptu party.
2. Make cakes to sell at a fundraising event.
3. Read books such as *Spot Bakes a Cake* by Eric Hill or *Kipper's Birthday* by Mick Inkpen.

Links to Foundation Stage Curriculum

PSE Work as part of a group or class, taking turns and sharing fairly, understanding that there need to be agreed values and codes of behaviour for groups of people, including adults and children, to work together harmoniously

MD Order two items by weight or capacity (SS)

ELG Use language such as 'greater', 'smaller', 'heavier' or 'lighter' to compare quantities

KUW Show an awareness of change (SS)

ELG Ask questions about why things happen and how things work

Health and safety

⚠ Hygiene issues such as handwashing
⚠ Ensure hands are kept away from mouths and faces
⚠ Adults only to have access to cooker
⚠ Be aware of food allergies

ACTIVITY 6 Pasta collage

Resources you will need

- Sheets of medium-weight paper for each child
- PVA glue
- Spatulas
- Containers of uncooked pasta shapes

Aim/concept

- To use imagination and have fun

Process

- Show the children the pasta shapes and ask them what they can tell you about them.
- Who eats pasta? What do the children like about it? What do they eat with it? and so on.
- Let the children handle the pasta. What does it feel like? How does it compare to when it is cooked?
- Provide each child with paper and a spatula, and let them create a collage.
- Explain that pasta needs quite a generous amount of glue to ensure that it holds securely.

Vocabulary/discussion

- Refer to shapes using words such as spirals, tubes, twists, shells
- Use descriptive terms such as crunchy, hard, brittle
- Encourage discussion of texture: ridged, knobbly, lumpy

Group size

6–8

Links to Foundation Stage Curriculum

KUW Show curiosity, observe and manipulate objects and events (SS)

ELG Investigate objects and materials by using all of their senses as appropriate

CD Make constructions, collages, paintings, drawings and dances (SS)

ELG Explore colour, texture, shape, form and space in two or three dimensions

Extension ideas

1. Provide a bowl of mixed pasta shapes, and ask the children to classify them by shape (see page 66).
2. Allow the children to explore bowls of both cooked and uncooked pasta, then encourage them to make comparisons.
3. Let them take 'rubbings' of their pasta pictures.

Health and safety

⚠ Ensure that the pasta is not eaten
⚠ If using spaghetti, it should be kept away from eyes

ACTIVITY 7

The food shop

Resources you will need

- A low table to act as the counter
- A till, some money (real coins are always better than toy money)
- Sturdy cardboard boxes for displaying the goods
- A range of food boxes, toy or made fruits, vegetables, breads
- Shopping baskets
- Paper and pens for signs and shopping lists

Aim/concept

- To sort food by type, and share in a role-play activity

Process

- In advance, ask the children to bring in food packets and boxes.
- Set out all the items together, along with a range of pretend foods.
- Explain that you are going to make a shop and ask the children what they can tell you about shopping and selecting foods from supermarket shelves and markets.
- Encourage the children to sort foods into categories. Agree these with them in advance (e.g. greengroceries, bakery items).
- Help the children to stock their shelves.
- Help the children to write signs for the foods and then let them play, taking turns to buy and sell.
- Talk to the children about the foods they are selling/buying. What do they know about each item? Which have they tried? What do they like and dislike?
- Encourage the children to write shopping lists.

Vocabulary/discussion

- Discuss food types: fresh, frozen, baked
- Name and discuss food shops/areas: greengrocers, bakers, butchers, grocers
- Encourage description of taste, texture and smell
- Where do foods come from? How do they grow?
- How are foods produced?
- Encourage the counting of food items and of coins
- Discuss the difference between supermarket produce and (farmers') market produce: local, fresh, often soil still on roots.

Group size

4

Extension ideas

1. Add prices to the foods (1p, 2p, 5p, 10p) and help children pay and receive change, while developing their understanding of number values up to 10.
2. Provide a globe and discuss where foods are grown, and how they reach us.
3. Read stories such as *Don't Forget the Bacon* by Pat Hutchins.
4. Play games such as 'I went shopping, and in my basket I placed a _____', each child repeating the sentence in turn, adding an extra food item to the list.

Links to Foundation Stage Curriculum

CLL	Ascribe meanings to marks (SS)
ELG	Attempt writing for different purposes, using features of different forms such as lists, stories and instructions
CLL	Use talk, actions and objects to recall and relive past events (SS)
ELG	Use language to imagine and recreate roles and experiences
MD	Willingly attempt to count, with some numbers in the correct order (SS)
ELG	Count reliably up to 10 everyday objects
MD	Recognise numerals 1 to 5, then 1 to 9 (SS)
ELG	Recognise numerals 1 to 9
CD	Engage in imaginative and role play based on own first-hand experiences (SS)
ELG	Use their imagination in art and design, music, dance, imaginative and role-play stories

Health and safety

⚠ Ensure all packets and boxes are clean
⚠ Wash hands after handling real money
⚠ Remind younger children not to put coins in their mouths

ACTIVITY 8 **Marble cake**

Resources you will need

- A square or rectangular-shaped cake tin
- Mixing bowls
- Wooden spoons
- Scales, or measuring cups
- Ingredients for making cakes, as set out in recipe – page 93
- Cocoa
- Pink and green food colouring

Aim/concept

- To observe the way in which the different coloured cake mixtures blend during the baking process

Process

- Take the children to wash their hands. Be seen to wash yours too.
- Talk to the children about marble designs. Have they seen them on items such as work surfaces? Have they ever played with marbles? What have they noticed about the colours?
- Show the children examples of marbling effects.
- Talk to the children about making cake mixtures. How do they think they could make the same effect in their cake?
- Ask the children what they think might happen if they add colouring to the cake mixture. Explain this is what they are going to be doing.
- Make the cake mixture with the children, using the recipe on page 93, dividing the ingredients between three bowls.
- In one bowl, let the children add cocoa.
- In another, let the children add food colouring.
- In the third bowl, the mixture remains plain, or a third food colour may be added.
- Help the children to tip their mixtures into the prepared cake tin, making sure each mixture is tipped into a different area of the tin.
- Let the children who have made the plain mixture draw a swirl in the mixture, using a blunt knife.
- Cook the cake, and when cool, let the children slice it up and observe the marbled effect inside.

Vocabulary/discussion

- Encourage vocabulary linked to naming and discussing ingredients
- Talk about the changes to the mixture during the cooking process
- Use terms such as dry, liquid, runny, thickened, combined, altered, marbled
- Encourage discussion of taste. Do the different coloured parts of the cake taste the same or different? Which do they like best?

Group size

3 or 6 (if 2 to a bowl)

Links to Foundation Stage Curriculum

PSE Have a positive approach to new experiences (SS)

ELG Continue to be interested, excited and motivated to learn

KUW Show an awareness of change (SS)

ELG Ask questions about why things happen and how things work

CD Explore what happens when they mix colours (SS)

ELG Explore colour, texture, shape, form and space in two or three dimensions

Extension ideas

1. Provide a range of different coloured doughs for the children to blend as they wish.
2. Offer 'marbling' paint activities.
3. Provide 'marbled' mashed potato at lunchtime by adding food colours.
4. Make 'special eggs' (see page 32).

Health and safety

⚠ Observe hygiene issues such as handwashing
⚠ Ensure hands are kept away from mouths and faces
⚠ Only adults to have access to cooker
⚠ Be aware of food allergies, particularly when using food colouring

ACTIVITY

9 Fruit kebabs

Resources you will need

- A variety of fruits (e.g. peaches, bananas, strawberries, cherries (stones removed), grapes (seedless), melon, mango, pineapple)
- A sharp knife – adult use only
- Rounded-ended knives for the children to use
- Chopping boards
- Cocktail sticks or kebab skewers
- Large plate

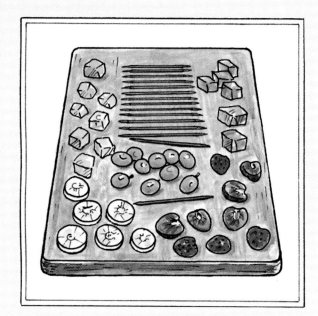

Aim/concept

- To select fruit and make their own fruit kebab

Process

- Display the range of fruits and discuss them with the children.
- What do the children know about them? Which have they tried? What are their favourites?
- Take the children to wash their hands. Be seen to wash yours too.
- Show the children how to cut the fruits into bite-size pieces.
- Let the children cut the softer fruits.
- Cut the firmer fruits for them.
- Demonstrate how to carefully thread pieces of fruit on to cocktail sticks or skewers to make a 'kebab'.
- Encourage the children to select their own kebab, counting and alternating the fruit, or making a repeated pattern if using the longer skewers.
- Enjoy eating the kebabs, discussing taste and texture.

Vocabulary/discussion

- Name the fruits
- Discuss colours, shapes, and where and how they are grown
- Encourage counting and discussion of patterns made with the fruit pieces
- Use positional language: The cherry is in front of the pineapple, the strawberry is next to the pear, the grapes are behind the melon
- Compare their kebabs with others'. What is the same? What difference can they see?
- Which fruits are sweetest? Which do they like best?

Group size

6

Links to Foundation Stage Curriculum

MD	Observe and use positional language (SS)
ELG	Use everyday words to describe position
PD	Understand that tools and equipment have to be used safely (SS)
ELG	Handle tools, objects construction and malleable materials safely and with increasing control
CD	Make comparisons (SS)
ELG	Express and communicate their ideas, thoughts and feelings

Extension ideas

1. Make cocktail kebabs for parties or picnics (see page 76).
2. Make rockets, using a cherry for the nosecone.
3. Make a fruit salad (see page 38).

Health and safety

- ⚠ Care should be taken with children using knives
- ⚠ Sharpest knife for adult use only
- ⚠ Ensure children understand the need to be careful with cocktail sticks
- ⚠ Be aware of food allergies

ACTIVITY 10 Peppermint creams

Resources you will need

- Two Large bowls
- Medium-size bowl for each child
- Whisk
- Sieve
- Food preparation board for each child
- Blunt knife for each child
- *Petit four* cases

Ingredients
225 g (8 oz) icing sugar
$1/4$ teaspoon cream of tartar
The white of one medium-size egg
A few drops of peppermint essence
A few drops of green food colouring (optional)

Aim/concept

- To mix and knead ingredients to prepare a simple treat

Process

- Take the children to wash their hands. Be seen to wash yours too.
- Ensure that the work surface or activity table is spotlessly clean.
- Talk to the children about sweets. What are their favourites? What type of sweets do they prefer (toffees, fruits, mints, chocolate)?
- Explain to the children that they are going to make peppermint creams. Has anyone had them before?
- Show the children how to whisk an egg-white in a large bowl. Ensure that the white is frothy and thick.
- Help the children to weigh and sieve the icing sugar and cream of tartar into the other large bowl.
- Help the children to add the egg-white gradually to the icing sugar, together with a few drops of peppermint essence.
- Let the children blend the ingredients together until the mixture forms a firm dough which is not sticky.
- Divide the mixture between the children.
- Add green food colouring to the mixture (optional).

- Let the children knead the peppermint dough well.
- Let each child sprinkle some icing sugar on to their board and encourage them to roll the dough into a sausage shape.
- Show the children how to cut the 'sausage' into 1 cm slices using the blunt knives.
- Place each peppermint cream into a paper case.
- Leave to dry for a while and then ENJOY!

Vocabulary/discussion

- Use terms such as whisk, mix, blend, knead, roll
- Talk about the changes noted in whisking the egg-white: runny, frothy, thickened

Group size

4

Extension ideas

1. Dip the peppermint creams in melted chocolate for an extra special treat.
2. 'Sell' the sweets at snack time or enjoy at party time.
3. Make peppermint faces, using tiny chocolate drops as features.

Links to Foundation Stage Curriculum

KUW Talk about what is seen and what is happening (SS)

ELG Ask questions about why things happen and how things work

PD Show awareness of a range of healthy practices with regard to eating, sleeping and hygiene (SS)

ELG Recognise the importance of keeping healthy and those things which contribute to this

Health and safety

⚠ Hygiene issues such as handwashing and clean boards
⚠ Care to be taken when using knives
⚠ Be aware of food allergies, especially if using food colouring

ACTIVITY 11 Designing a plate of healthy food

Resources you will need

- Paper plates
- Pictures of food from magazines and food packets
- Child-size scissors
- Pots of glue
- Spatulas

Aim/concept

- To design a healthy meal through creativity

Process

- In advance, ask the children to bring in a range of food pictures to share.
- Provide each child with a paper plate and scissors.
- Talk to the children about healthy and less healthy foods.
- Show the children pictures of food items in the four main food groups (see page 5).
- Encourage the children to select and cut out food items to stick on to their 'plate'. You may have to help some children with the cutting.
- Talk to the children about their chosen 'meals'. Why have they chosen those foods? Which are their favourites? What do they like about them? Which food groups do they belong to?
- Children may be allowed a free choice, or given a theme for their plate (e.g a party, Christmas dinner).
- Display the filled up plates.

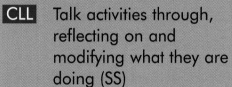

Vocabulary/ discussion

- Talk about healthy eating and the need to eat a balanced amount of foods from each of the main food groups
- Talk about types of food and when they might be eaten. Ask children about their favourite foods, flavours, textures
- Discuss cooked and uncooked foods, packaging of foods, what happens to packages afterwards

Group size

6–8

Extension ideas

1. Link activity to a general theme about food.
2. Link to a topic on waste and recycling.
3. Let the children plan their meals and then 'buy' their foods from a 'shop' first (see page 44).
4. Make a giant-sized plate and divide it into four sections. Encourage the children to select food from each of the four main foods.
5. Provide books about food for the children to explore.
6. Read stories linked to food (e.g. *Oliver's Vegetables* by Vivian French, and *Don't Forget the Bacon* by Pat Hutchins).

Links to Foundation Stage Curriculum

CLL Talk activities through, reflecting on and modifying what they are doing (SS)

ELG Use talk to organise, sequence and clarify thinking, ideas, feelings and events

KUW Describe simple features of objects and events (SS)

ELG Find out about, and identify, some features of living things, objects and events they observe

CD Work creatively on a large or small scale (SS)

ELG Explore colour, texture, shape, form and space in two or three dimensions

Health and safety

⚠ Careful supervision of scissor use
⚠ Ensure all food packages are clean

ACTIVITY 12 Making a favourite food book

Resources you will need

- An A4 sheet of paper for each child
- Pens
- Crayons
- Pictures of food from magazines
- Scissors
- Spatulas
- Glue
- Biscuit boxes

Aim/concept

- Children to record their favourite foods through a creative activity

Process

- *Either* demonstrate how to fold the sheet of paper into a miniature book (see page 95), *or* have the 'books' ready folded.
- Talk to the children about books, discussing the need for a title-page, author's name and so on.
- Explain that they are going to make a book about food.
- Ensure that the children have their books the right way up in front of them before they begin.
- Explain that they can choose the food theme for their book: favourite foods, fruits, vegetables, sweets and so on.
- Provide a range of pictures for the children to cut out and use if they choose, and pens for them to draw their own food items and write their name and book title.
- Provide sample 'book titles' such as 'Fruits', 'Vegetables' and so on for the more able children to copy.
- Use firm-sided biscuit boxes to display the books as a mini library.
- Encourage the children to share their books with each other during group time.

Vocabulary/discussion

- In making the books, use terms such as fold, flatten, line up, open, display, title, author
- Discuss names and origins of food items with the children, according to their choices

Group size

6–8

Links to Foundation Stage Curriculum

CLL Know that information may be relayed in the form of print (SS)

ELG Know that print carries meaning and, in English, is read from left to right and from top to bottom

PD Manipulate materials to achieve a planned effect (SS)

ELG Handle tools, objects, construction and malleable materials safely and with increasing control.

CD Make three-dimensional structures (SS)

ELG Explore colour, texture, shape, form and space in two or three dimensions

Extension ideas

1. Link to a topic on health, encouraging the children to make books showing only healthy foods.
2. Make a giant food wheel, showing the main food groups and what items go where (see page 5).
3. Make recipe books for favourite items such as cakes, illustrating a different ingredient on each page.
4. Provide a range of food magazines for discussion.
5. Use children's recipe books when cooking with children, encouraging them to follow the instructions.

Health and safety

⚠ Careful supervision of scissor use
⚠ Non-toxic glues

13 Bird seed cake

Resources you will need

- Pictures of garden birds, and bird feeders
- A tub of vegetable fat
- Sunflower seeds
- Crushed peanuts
- Thistle seed
- Mixed birdseed
- Containers to present the above 'ingredients'
- A large mixing bowl
- Empty plastic bowls with four holes already made in the base
- Metal tablespoons
- String or old shoe-laces – two lengths for each child

Aim/concept

- To raise awareness of the need to provide food for birds, and to enjoy mixing a range of nutritious ingredients together.

Process

- Discuss the pictures of garden birds with the children. What do they know about them? Why do the birds need feeding?
- Talk about the types of food birds like to eat, explaining why large items such as whole peanuts should only be placed in feeders so that they cannot be given whole by adults to their young, who might choke on them.
- Let the children handle the various seeds and encourage them to describe how they look, smell and feel.
- Encourage each child to help blend the ingredients, spooning the fat into the mixing bowl and gradually adding the various seeds and crushed nuts.
- Ensure that the mixture is evenly mixed.
- Give each child a bowl and two lengths of string. Show them how to thread them through the holes so that all the ends are roughly equal, hanging underneath the bowl.
- Explain to the children that they need to open the strings out and then add large spoonfuls of the bird food to their bowl, packing it down firmly.
- Explain to the children why it is important to continue to provide food for birds once you have started. Issues of responsibility.
- Bowls may either be taken home or hung around the outdoor environment and observed for bird activity.

Vocabulary/discussion

- Discuss the reasons why we feed birds, especially in winter
- Encourage the children to describe what they are seeing and doing

Group size

6–8

Links to Foundation Stage Curriculum

PSE Show care and concern for others, for living things and for the environment (SS)

ELG Consider the consequences of their words and actions for themselves and others

KUW Show an interest in the world in which they live (SS)

ELG Observe, find out about and identify features in the place they live and the natural world

KUW Examine objects and living things to find out more about them (SS)

ELG Find out about, and identify, some features of living things, objects and events they observe

Extension ideas

1. Link to a topic on birds, wildlife or gardens.
2. Provide other bird feeders and let the children top them up regularly.
3. Encourage the children to observe and record the birds' visits.
4. Talk about nests and how they are made, and what from.

Health and safety

⚠ Ensure that no child eats the seeds or crushed nuts
⚠ Be aware of allergies (you may need to avoid using nuts altogether)

ACTIVITY

14 Scented dough

Resources you will need

- Appropriate ingredients to make one of the dough recipes on pages 11–14
- Small containers of different scents and essences (e.g. lemon essence, peppermint essence)
- Cocoa
- Strong liquid coffee
- Lavender water (eau-de-toilette)
- Rose-water

Aim/concept

- To explore dough using both smell and texture

Process

- Make up the dough according to the selected recipe.
- If using the cooked dough, prepare in advance and allow to cool.
- Ask the children to smell the dough before anything has been added. What does it smell like?
- Present the range of mystery 'smells' in small containers or sprinklers.
- Let each child choose one smell to add to their portion of dough.
- Encourage the children to knead the dough well.
- Can the children guess what they have added to their dough?
- Encourage the children to guess what has been added to each portion of dough in turn. It may help if they wash their hands thoroughly before trying this part of the activity to eradicate the smell of the dough.
- Display the portions of dough on plates on a table. Try mixing the plates up regularly. Who can guess the different smells now?
- Ask the children to group the 'smells' as sweet, sour and so on.

Vocabulary/discussion

- Describe smells – sour, sweet, bitter, mild, strong, perfumed, flowery

Group size

1 per smell, maximum of 8

Extension ideas

1. Link to a topic on our senses.
2. Play – What can you smell? (See page 34).
3. Prepare information cards, naming each smell. Include a picture for younger children. Who can match the card to the right smell?

Links to Foundation Stage Curriculum

CLL	Know that information may be relayed in the form of print (SS)
ELG	Know that print carries meaning and, in English, is read from left to right and top to bottom
CLL	Begin to recognise some familiar words (SS)
ELG	Read a range of familiar and common words and simple sentences independently
KUW	Describe simple features of objects and events (SS)
ELG	Investigate objects and materials by using all the senses as appropriate
CD	Further explore an experience using a range of senses (SS)
SS	Make comparisons (SS)
ELG	Respond in a variety of ways to what they see, hear, smell, touch and feel

Health and safety

⚠ Be aware of food and skin allergies
⚠ Explain to the children that the scents and essences are not to be eaten or drunk
⚠ Ensure that hands are washed thoroughly after the activity

ACTIVITY 15 Printing with fruits and vegetables

Resources you will need

- Aprons
- Sheets of paper
- Shallow containers of paint
- Thin layers of sponge (optional) to cover the base of the containers
- A variety of halved fruits and vegetables: potatoes, peppers, carrots (cut lengthways), large mushrooms, cauliflower florets, apples, pears, star fruits, pomegranates
- A sharp knife – for adult use only

Aim/concept

- To explore the shape and texture of fruits and vegetables with paint

Process

- Explain to the children what the activity is going to involve.
- Ask the children to name the fruits and vegetables, and to tell you what they know about each one.
- Explain that fruits and vegetables are an important source of vitamins and are needed to keep us healthy (see page 5).
- Talk about the shapes and ask the children to think what they might look like when you cut them in half. Encourage them to use description.
- Cut each item of food into two in turn, showing the two halves to the children and discussing what they see.
- Help the children to make comparisons, noting similarities and differences.
- Encourage the children to make a painting by printing with the fruit and vegetable halves by dipping them in the dishes of paint.
- Display the paintings.

Vocabulary/ discussion

- Names of fruits and vegetables
- Talk about vitamins and how these contribute to good health
- Colours and shapes of fruits and vegetables
- Words such as halve, divide, split, equal
- Words such as seed, core, stalk, stem, floret, skin, flesh, pip, firm, hard
- Introduce comparative language such as similar to, the same as, compare, resemble

Group size

4–6

Extension ideas

1. Link to a general topic on fruit and vegetables, shopping or healthy eating.
2. Play the game 'I went shopping and in my basket I put...', each child repeating what has been said and adding another item to the basket as the game moves from person to person.
3. Fold a sheet of paper into four sections (or draw divisions with a pen), then print a different fruit or vegetable in each 'quarter', making an identifying game for others to play.
4. Print using potatoes cut in half with raised shapes cut into them (e.g. square, triangle).

Links to Foundation Stage Curriculum

KUW Sort objects by one function (SS)

ELG Look closely at similarities, differences, patterns and change

PD Show awareness of a range of healthy practices with regard to eating, sleeping and hygiene (SS)

ELG Recognise the importance of keeping healthy and those things which contribute to this.

CD Work creatively on a large or small scale (SS)

ELG Explore colour, texture, shape, form and space in 2 or 3D

Health and safety

⚠ Be aware of any allergies to the fruits and vegetables you use

⚠ Keep the sharp knife safely away from the children

ACTIVITY 16 Making fruit smoothies

Resources you will need

- A variety of soft fruits: strawberries, raspberries, loganberries and bananas are ideal
- Shallow bowls, one for each child
- Milk – enough for a drink for each child
- A 'special' glass (or plastic tumbler) for each child
- A small jug for each child
- Sieves
- Metal tablespoons
- Swizzle sticks to stir with
- Chocolate and small grater (optional)

Aim/concept

- To enjoy making a luxury drink for a snack or party time

Process

- Talk about milk, Who enjoys milk smoothies?, and the flavours the children like best.
- Let the children name the fruits and describe their taste, smell and shape.
- Using sieves and spoons, each child crushes their chosen fruit into a bowl. Adult help may be needed here.
- Help each child to pour some milk into their jug.
- Encourage them to spoon the sieved fruit into their jug of milk and stir it well.
- Help them to pour the smoothie mixture back through the sieve into their glass.
- Sprinkle surface of drink with grated chocolate (optional).
- Provide them with a swizzle stick to stir the smoothie while they enjoy their drink.

Vocabulary/discussion

- Discuss names and features of each fruit
- Discuss changes in the fruits, their texture and so on once the fruits have been crushed or sieved
- When have the children had smoothies in the past?
- What other fruits could they use?

Group size

4–6

Extension ideas

1. Prepare in advance and refrigerate for a party.
2. Cut out appropriate shapes and paint filled Sundae glasses for a wall display or for outside a café role-play area.
3. Read *Oliver's Milkshake* by Vivian French.

Links to Foundation Stage Curriculum

PSE Display high levels of involvement in activities (SS)

ELG Continue to be interested, excited and motivated to learn

KUW Describe simple features of objects and events (SS)

ELG Investigate objects and materials by using all their senses as appropriate

PD Use simple tools to effect changes to the materials (SS)

ELG Handle tools, objects, construction and malleable materials safely and with increasing control

Health and safety

⚠ Be aware of food allergies (especially strawberries and kiwifruit)

⚠ Provide soya milk for children who cannot drink cows' milk

ACTIVITY

17 Simple pizzas

Resources you will need

- Access to a grill or oven – adult use only
- A saucer
- Round-ended knives
- Tablespoons
- Baking trays – already lightly greased
- A slice of bread for each child
- Tomato ketchup (or tomato purée)
- Grated cheese
- Optional items as extras (e.g mushrooms, peppers, olives, anchovies, pineapple pieces)

Aim/concept

- To make a simple pizza for lunch or snack time

Process

- Ask who likes pizza and what sort they enjoy best.
- Do the children know where pizzas originate from? Has anyone been to Italy?
- Can the children show you Italy on a map or globe?
- Show the children your range of ingredients. Can they work out how to make a pizza? Let them tell you.
- Take the children to wash their hands. Be seen to wash yours too.
- Show the children how to press a saucer on to their slice of bread and cut around it using a rounded-ended knife. You may need to do this for them.
- Let the children spread tomato sauce or ketchup over their circle of bread.
- Let the children spoon grated cheese on to the top and spread it out.
- Let them choose their extra topping (optional).
- Place under the grill or in a pre-heated oven, and grill/bake until the cheese melts and the bread is lightly toasted.
- The pizza circles are ready to eat once they have cooled slightly.

Vocabulary/discussion

- Talk about Italy. Where is it? What do the children know about it? Can they find it on a map or globe?
- Discuss pizza toppings: favourite flavours, textures and smells
- Describe actions in making a pizza – using a template, cutting around it, spreading, grating, choosing the topping.

Group size

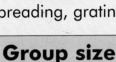

2–4

Extension ideas

1. Find Italy on a map or a globe. Then find the countries of each child's homeland.
2. Talk about famous places in Italy – Venice, Florence, Pisa
3. What famous places can the children think of in their homeland? Be ready to prompt them.
4. Talk about holidays. Who has been to Italy? Where did they visit?
5. Colour in Italian flags – green, white and red blocks of colour.
6. Make pizza faces, using olives or slices of pepper (see page 77).
7. Make ladybird pizzas, using olives and anchovies.

Links to Foundation Stage Curriculum

PSE Have a sense of self as a member of different communities (SS)

ELG Have a developing respect for their own cultures and beliefs and those of other people

KUW Gain an awareness of the cultures and beliefs of others (SS)

ELG Begin to learn about their own cultures and beliefs and those of other people

PD Engage in activities requiring hand–eye coordination (SS)

ELG Handle tools, objects, construction and malleable materials safely and with increasing control

Health and safety

⚠ Ensure hands are well washed
⚠ Careful supervision of knife use
⚠ Be aware of food allergies

ACTIVITY 18 Classifying with pasta

Resources you will need

- Pasta of all shapes, colours and sizes
- Sectioned trays for sorting the pasta (party 'nibbles' trays are good for this)
- *Or provide a classifying wheel (see photocopiable sheet on page 92)*

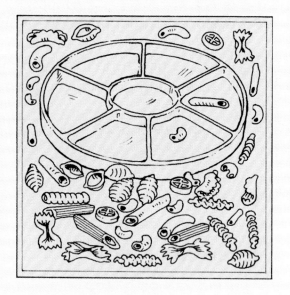

Aim/concept

- To classify pasta shapes by one or more features

Process

- Provide a large quantity of uncooked pasta for the children to sort.
- Encourage the children to first describe each type, its colour, shape and size. Which are the largest? smallest? thinnest?
- Let the children handle it and make patterns.
- Who can make a repeating pattern?
- Explain that the sorting trays are for the children to classify the pasta shapes.
- Encourage the children to ask each other for shapes using description.
- Encourage them to count the shapes during and after the activity.
- Try limiting the numbers of pasta shapes, encouraging the children to divide them into groups, and count each group both separately and together, emphasising how two groups may be added together.

Vocabulary/discussion

- Discuss shape, colour and size
- Count with the children
- Encourage positional language (e.g. the green shell is next to . . . , the white twists are on top of . . .)

Group size

6–8 depending on amount of pasta available

Extension ideas

1. Provide laminated A4 sheets numbered 1 to 9 for the children to count the pasta shapes on to.
2. Make a pasta collage (see page 42).
3. Present activity when there is pasta for lunch, and discuss the difference between cooked and uncooked pasta.

Links to Foundation Stage Curriculum

CLL Have emerging self-confidence to speak to others about ambitions and interests (SS)

ELG Interact with others, negotiating plans and activities and taking turns in conversations

MD Use mathematical language in play (SS)

ELG Say and use number names in order in familiar contexts

MD Find the total number of items in two groups by counting all of them

ELG Begin to relate addition to combining two groups of objects and subtraction to 'taking away'

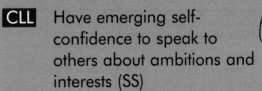

Health and safety

⚠ Be aware of food allergies
⚠ Explain that the pasta is not for eating, as it has been handled too much.

ACTIVITY 19 Making vegetable soup

Resources you will need

- A chopping board for each child
- Potato peelers
- Medium sharp knives
- Polystyrene cups with lids
- A small spoon for each child
- A large saucepan
- A large bowl
- A ladle
- Access to a cooker – adults only
- A range of vegetables: potatoes, carrots, celery, swede, turnip, broccoli, a leek plus some peas (fresh if possible), enough of each for a small portion for each child.
- A tin of low-salt tomato soup, or a low-salt vegetable stock cube.

Aim/concept

- To learn how to prepare vegetables for cooking, and treating utensils with respect.

Process

- Take the children to wash their hands. Be seen to wash yours too.
- Talk about the vegetables, and demonstrate how to remove their outer skins through peeling as appropriate.
- Let each child peel part of a vegetable, explaining the importance of taking care with sharp utensils. You may need to help them with this.
- Demonstrate how to cut the vegetables up safely, and give the children thick slices of swede, potato and so on to cut into small pieces.
- Encourage the children to 'swap' vegetable pieces so that everyone has tried to cut up as many different vegetables as time allows.
- Let each child pod some fresh peas (if available).
- Encourage the children to discuss the smells and textures of the vegetables during the preparation process.
- If possible, have enough vegetables for the children to eat small pieces raw. How do they describe them?
- Ask the children to place their prepared vegetables into the saucepan and add the soup or stock, everyone stirring it well.
- Explain that you will now put the soup on to cook. Talk to the children about this, explaining the difference between boiling and simmering.

- Let the soup come to the boil and then turn down the heat, leaving it to simmer for about 20 minutes (or until the vegetables have softened).
- Pour into a large bowl and leave safely to cool down a little.
- When cooled sufficiently to be safe for the children, help them each to ladle themselves a portion into a polystyrene cup.
- Either drink the soup with a spoon as a snack, or add a lid and take home for lunch.
- Talk about the changes seen in the vegetables.

Vocabulary/discussion

- Encourage and introduce descriptive language – hard, rough, hairy, starchy, pungent, sweet
- Help the children to describe the preparation processes – cutting, slicing, peeling, paring, podding
- Talk about the difference between boiling and simmering. What else is cooked/made using these methods (e.g. the kettle to make tea)?

Group size

4

Extension ideas

1. Shop with the children to buy the vegetables in advance.
2. Make print designs with the same types of vegetables (see page 60).
3. Read books such as *The Enormous Turnip*, a traditional tale.
4. Grow vegetable toppings on a window-sill (see page 70).

Links to Foundation Stage Curriculum

CLL Extend vocabulary, especially by grouping and naming (SS)

ELG Extend their vocabulary, exploring the meanings and sounds of new words

KUW Describe simple features of objects and events (SS)

ELG Investigate objects and materials by using all their senses as appropriate

PD Understand that equipment and tools have to be used safely (SS)

ELG Handle tools, objects, construction and malleable materials safely and with increasing control

Health and safety

⚠ Careful supervision of children using knives
⚠ Ensure soup is not given to the children while too hot
⚠ Adults only to use cooker
⚠ Be aware of food allergies

ACTIVITY 20 Growing vegetable tops

Resources you will need

- A carrot with its long ferns still attached (initially keep this out of sight)
- Flat dishes or old saucers
- Pieces of lint, or a similar absorbent material – layers of folded kitchen paper work well
- Carrots and parsnips, either with tiny amounts of greenery coming out of their tops, or which look very healthy
- Knives
- Small jug of water

Aim/concept

- To 'plant' and look after a sprouting vegetable, and measure its growth

Process

- Talk to the children about how the vegetables grow. How do we know they are there when they are underground and so on?
- You may wish to use the photocopiable sheet on page 85 in advance.
- Show the children the carrot with the long ferns still attached.
- Explain to the children that they are going to 'grow' the carrot and parsnip tops using the resources in front of them. Can they work out what they need to do?
- Discuss their ideas with the children.
- Demonstrate how to cut the vegetables safely, and supervise the children as they do this.
- Let the children assemble the lint and vegetable tops into the dishes and add a little water.
- Explain to the children that they must check their vegetable plants each day, and water them to keep the lint moist. They can also measure their vegetables regularly.
- Allow the children to put their vegetables somewhere light where they can access them easily. A window-sill is ideal.
- Look at the vegetables daily with the children and discuss and measure their growth.

Vocabulary/discussion

- Talk about issues of responsibility (care, attention, observation) and also about need (water, sunlight, space). Explore what the children think are their own needs for healthy growth
- When measuring the growing plants, use mathematical language to describe height and numbers of leaves, and make comparisons between the plants: tallest, shortest, fastest growing, largest leaves, thinnest leaves and so on

Group size

6–8

Links to Foundation Stage Curriculum

PSE Show care and concern for others, for living things and for the environment

ELG Consider the consequences of their words and actions for themselves and others

MD Order two or three items by length (SS)

ELG Use everyday words to describe position

KUW Examine objects and living things to find out more about them (SS)

ELG Find out about, and identify, some features of living things, objects and events they observe

Extension ideas

1. Make a chart to record the growth of the vegetables.
2. Link to making vegetable soup (see page 68).
3. Will any other vegetable tops sprout? Let the children try.
4. Use the photocopiable 'book' template on page 95 to make a planting sequence story.

Health and safety

⚠ Careful supervision of knife use

Meal and snack suggestions

Simple to prepare, inviting to eat

This section presents food ideas to help entice reluctant children to enjoy eating, and to prepare as special treats for all children. Ideas are given for making the following foods a little more interesting:

- Sandwiches
- Celery
- Tomatoes
- Salad onions
- Cucumber
- Eggs
- Fresh fruit
- Pastry
- Pizzas
- Toast

There are also a variety of interestingly named items:

- Hedgehog eggs
- Fresh fruit kebab rockets
- Traffic-lights
- Special treat fruit
- Decorated eggs
- Steam train sandwiches
- Fish finger wigwams
- Clown faces
- Fruity faces
- Bread and cheese beach

Not all children have a positive attitude to food, and some children are very unenthusiastic or choosy eaters. Some children receive a limited range of foods at home and become reluctant to try new tastes and textures, whereas others have been encouraged to try new items and are always keen to experiment.

Children's appetites vary enormously too, with some requiring far more to 'fill them up' than others. At times it can be concerning to see a child eat minimal amounts at each mealtime, and as early years practitioners we need to find ways to encourage children to eat a varied range of foods in sufficient amounts to give them the energy and nutrients for their healthy all-round development.

Children will often respond well to food which looks interesting, hence the recent trend for food manufacturers to produce shaped and multi-coloured food items for young children.

Using pastry cutters is the simplest form of providing novelty lunches for children who need a little more encouragement. The following meal and snack suggestions also offer simple ideas for setting food out attractively.

Sandwiches

Make sandwiches more attractive by cutting them into shapes: squares, triangles and rectangles are simple. Let the children choose their shapes. How many can they name?

Or:

Try using pastry cutters for extra special shapes and put the 'edges' out for the birds.

Celery

Provide small, narrow sticks of celery and little pots of cottage cheese or cream cheese for dipping into.

Spread cream cheese along celery sticks and dot with raisins.

Tomatoes

Cut tomatoes into water lily shapes, by using a serrated edge knife to cut a zigzag shape all around the middle. Pull the two halves apart to produce the water lily effect.

Cut large tomatoes in half, scoop out the middle, mix with cooled, cooked rice and chopped chives, and spoon back into tomato shells.

Salad onion reeds

Slice salad onions down their length and leave to stand in a glass of water for a short while. They will splay outwards like river reeds.

Cucumber wheels

Make six or seven cuts down the length of a cucumber, then slice thinly into wheel shapes.

Hedgehog eggs

Coat a hard-boiled egg with cream cheese and insert carrot sticks into it to make a hedgehog. Use raisins for the eyes.

Fresh fruit kebab rockets

Cut up small pieces of fruit and thread on to cocktail sticks or kebab skewers.

Better still, let the children enjoy making them (see page 48).

Pastry ideas

Make pastry cases as if for jam tarts but add whisked egg, with grated cheese and a little finely cut-up onion to make mini-quiches.

Or:

Add grated cheese to your usual pastry mix and cut into stars and other shapes.

Simple pizzas

Cut bread slices into circles (use a saucer as a guide). Spread with tomato sauce and sprinkle with grated cheese. Toast or oven bake lightly.

Better still, make these with the children (see page 64).

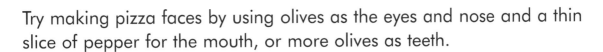

Try making pizza faces by using olives as the eyes and nose and a thin slice of pepper for the mouth, or more olives as teeth.

Or:

Make pizza ladybirds, using olives for the spots and anchovies for the legs.

Traffic lights

Make traffic lights by threading a green olive (or a green grape), a chunk of cheese and a mini tomato onto a cocktail stick.

Special toast fingers

Spread lightly toasted bread with marmite and top with grated cheese. Put back briefly under the grill.

Special treat fruit

Dip strawberries or chunks of banana into melted chocolate and put in the fridge to set. Yum!

Decorated eggs

Decorated eggs look lovely, and a child's involvement in the decorating process can entice them to eat the egg too.

Let children slice their eggs and make their own sandwich.

Try carrying out the activity 'Special eggs' on page 32 where the eggs have a lovely marbled effect, or alternatively encourage children to decorate their own eggs with pens.

Steam train sandwich

For each child you will need:

Two slices of bread
Margarine
Slices of tomato
Thin sticks of carrot
Grated cheese
Sultanas

Process

- Thinly spread the bread with margarine and make into a sandwich
- Cut the sandwich in half
- Use one half for the base of the train
- Cut the remaining half into two and position as the cab and truck
- Use tomato slices as wheels
- Position grated cheese as the steam
- Sultanas can be the cargo
- Join the wheels with the carrot sticks

Fish finger wigwams

For each child you will need:

Three fish fingers (or veggie fingers)
Mashed potato
Peas
Sticks of carrot

Process

- Mix the peas into the mashed potato
- Spoon the mashed potato mix into a pyramid shape
- Position the three fish fingers on a slant, at equal distances around the potato, making them touch at the top
- Make a 'campfire' outside the wigwam with the carrot sticks

Meal suggestion – Clown faces

For each child you will need:

A sausage
Half a tomato
A large mushroom, halved
Mashed potato, or mashed swede
Peas, baked beans or runner beans

Process

- Position the sausage as a mouth
- The mushroom and half a tomato form the eyes and nose
- The mashed potato (or swede) forms the sideburns
- The peas or beans form the hair

Try adding food colouring to mashed potato. Use different colours to achieve a marbled effect.

Fruity faces

You will need:

A thin slice of melon for each child
Grapes or sultanas
Kiwi or orange slices
Grape or cherry for the nose

Process

- Cut the melon along its length to form 'teeth'
- Position slices of kiwi or orange as 'eyes'
- Use the cherry or a grape for the nose
- Grapes or sultanas can form the 'hair'.

Bread and cheese beach

You will need:

A slice of bread for each child
Grated cheese
Pasta shells, cooked and cooled
A thin slice of celery stick
For best effect, set out on a blue plate (the sea)

Process

- Cut the slice of bread diagonally, cutting one half in half again
- Set out in yacht shape as shown below
- Use grated cheese as the sand
- Position the celery stick as the mast
- Pasta shells finish the picture off well

Photocopiable sheets

Bush or tree 'matching up' game

Can you draw a line from each fruit to where it grows?

Name _____ **Date** _____

Above or below ground 'matching up' game

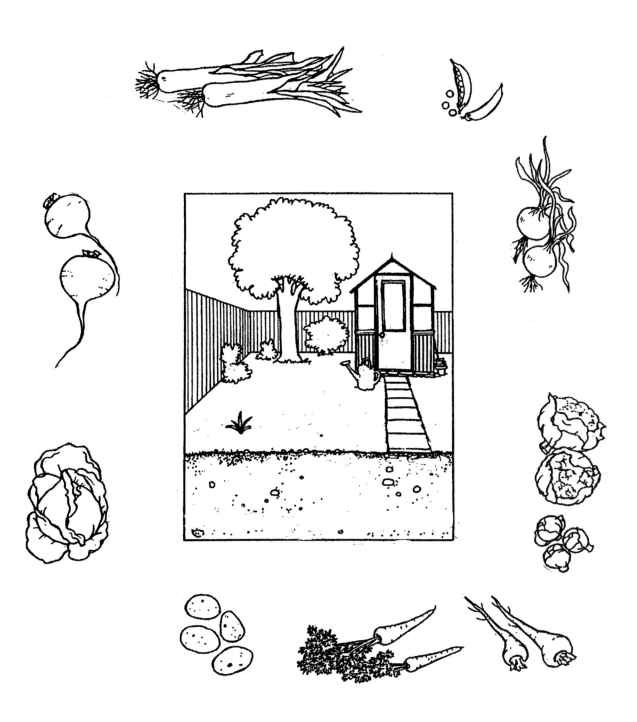

Can you draw a line from each vegetable to where it grows?

Name _____ **Date** _____

Source of food 'pairing up' game

Can you draw a line to show which food comes from which source?

Name _____ **Date** _____

Sequencing activity –
Making an ice-cream

Cut these pictures out and put them in the correct order to make an ice-cream.

Name _____ **Date** _____

Sequencing activity – Making cakes

Cut these pictures out and put them in the correct order to make cakes.

Name _____ **Date** _____

Six fruit shapes to colour appropriately

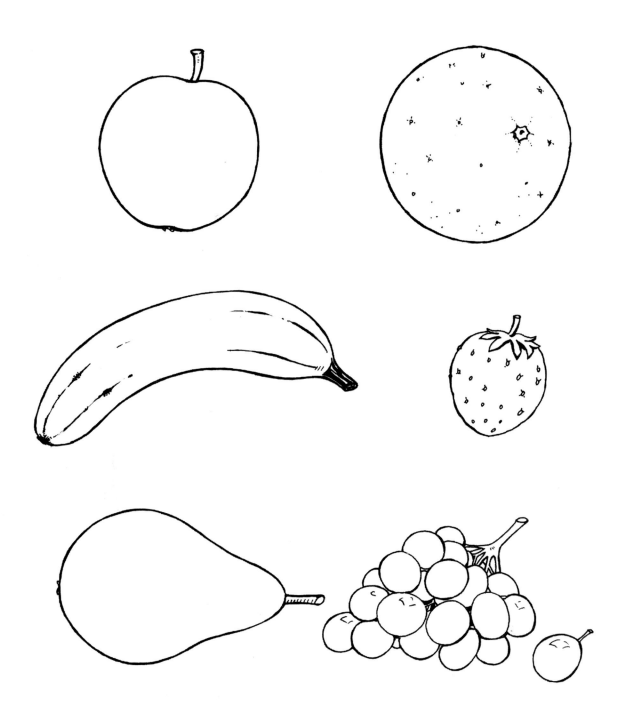

Can you colour the fruit in their natural colours?

Name _____ **Date** _____

Six vegetable shapes to colour appropriately

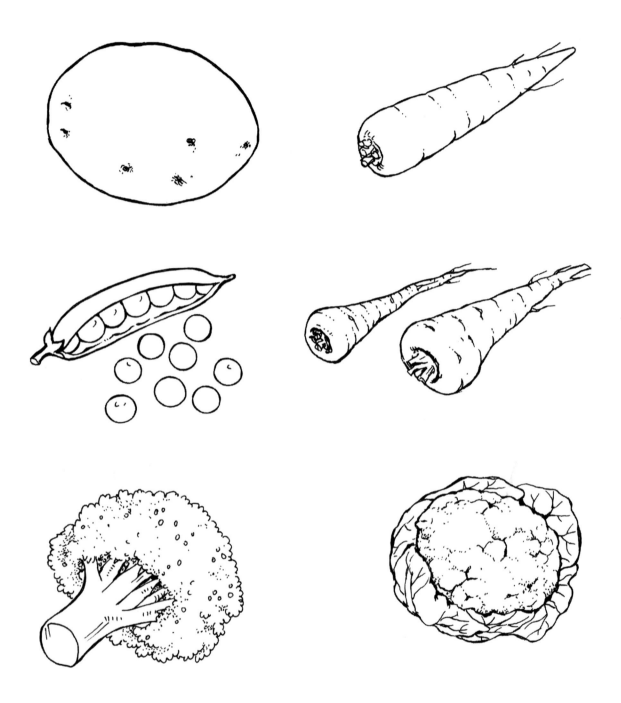

Can you colour the vegetables in their natural colours?

Name _____ **Date** _____

Outline of a cake to 'decorate'

How will you decorate your cake?

Name _____   **Date** _____

Template of a classifying wheel

(For best results enlarge this template to A3)

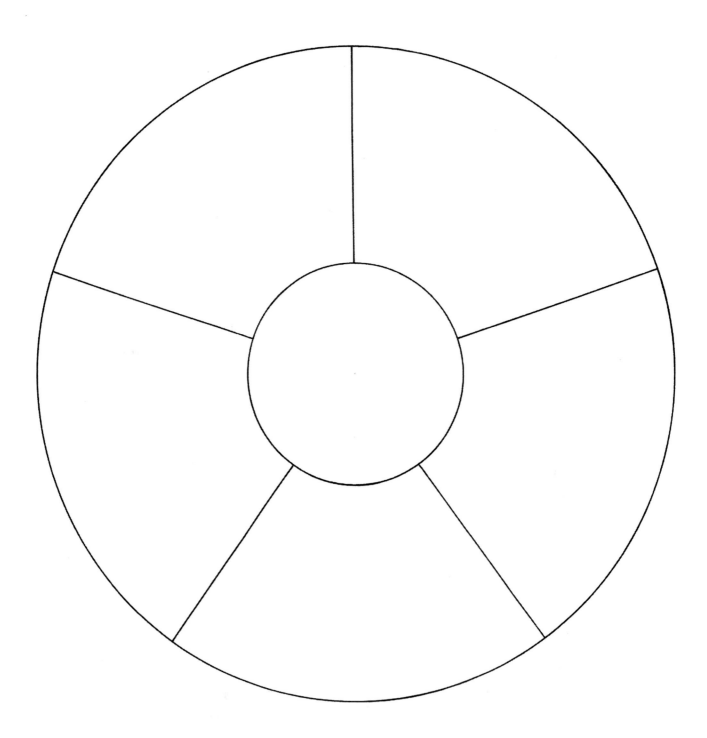

What will you put in each section?

Name _____ **Date** _____

A recipe for making cakes

Ingredients

112 g (4 oz) margarine
112 g (4 oz) sugar
2 eggs
225 g (8 oz) self-raising flour

Utensils needed

- Mixing bowl
- Wooden spoon
- Small bowls for ingredients
- Weighing scales
- Small whisk
- Bun tin
- Wire cooking rack

Method

1. Help the children weigh out the ingredients into different small bowls, placing the margarine in the main bowl.
2. Everyone to whisk the eggs.
3. Mix the sugar into the margarine until smooth and creamy.
4. Add the eggs, a little at a time.
5. Gradually add the flour and mix well.
6. Spoon mixture into the bun tins (or cake cases), *or* add food colouring if making marble cake (see page 46 for guidance).
7. Bake in a moderate oven for about 12 minutes.
8. Place on a wire rack to cool.
9. Decorate (optional) using ideas on page 94.
10. Enjoy!

Ideas for decorating cakes

Making a miniature book from an A4 sheet

1. An A4 sheet held landscape.

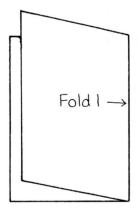

2. Fold the A4 sheet in half, with the fold on the right. Fold 1 →

3. Fold the two sides outwards towards the central fold. Open the furthest side out again. You should now have one layer of paper on the left and three on the right.

Fold 3 ←
Fold 2 →

4. Fold in half towards you.

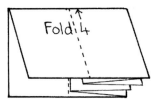

Fold 4

5. Open up again (as in stage 2 with fold again on your right). Cut half-way along the horizontal fold, from the right to the left.

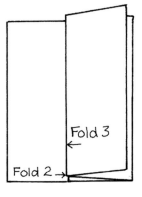

cut along ½ of fold 4

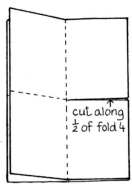

Fold

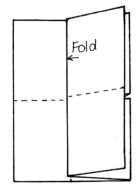

6. Fold as in stage 3. You should have one layer of paper on the left and three layers on the right.

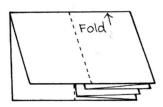

Fold

7. Fold in half downwards, towards you once again.

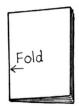

Fold

8. Fold in half again sideways to form a book shape.

References and suggested reading

Michael Bond, Paddington Bear books (Collins)

Vivian French, *Oliver's Fruit Salad* (Hodder Children's Books)

Vivian French, *Oliver's Milkshake* (Hodder Children's Books)

Vivian French, *Oliver's Vegetables* (Hodder Children's Books)

Sandy Green, *BTec National Early Years* (Nelson Thornes)

Heliadore (illustrator), *The Kitchen Garden* (Moonlight)

Eric Hill, *Spot Bakes a Cake* (Puffin)

Pat Hutchins, *Don't Forget the Bacon* (The Bodley Head)

Mick Inkpen, *Kipper's Birthday* (Hodder Children's Books)

John Vernon Lord and Janet Burroway, *The Giant Jam Sandwich* (Macmillan Children's Books)

The Caroline Walker Trust, *Eating Well for Under-5s in Child Care*

Traditional *The Enormous Turnip*

Charlotte Zolotow, *Mr Rabbit and the Lovely Present* (HarperCollins Picture Lions)